B & M Potterycrafts.

Tutorial on successful clay modelling.

OR

How to make it stick together.

Section 1. Why it didn't work.

Section 2. How to make it work.

Section 3. 'Good practice' techniques.

B & M Potterycrafts.

Tutorial on successful clay modelling.

Introduction.

The information in this tutorial was generated in response to a request from a teacher who had been tasked by her head teacher to train all her colleagues to work successfully with clay.

Her ceramics degree had not been of a practical nature and she was struggling to put the information together.

Putting the information down on paper had the effect of clarifying in my mind several things that I had done for years but had not considered why they worked.

I have included in this introduction section details of the simple tools and work surfaces that we have developed and used successfully over the years, you can make your own or buy similar versions in most craft shops.

The techniques outlined in the tutorial have served us in good stead and proven their worth working with school children, adults and students with special educational needs.

I have enjoyed producing this book and I hope that you enjoy reading and using it.

Enjoy your clay modelling.

Simple Clay Modelling Tools.

In this section I will outline which tools are needed to perform the tasks and skills described in the tutorial.

All the tools can be bought in craft or hobby shops or you can produce cheap alternatives which are just as good and in some cases better and more suitable for use in schools.

Modelling tools shown in this section are the simple tools needed for sculpting small models, most thumb pots and most coil pots.

The paint brush is chosen for its stiff bristles which allow you to rough up the clay to help with cross hatching or obviate the need for cross hatching in some circumstances.

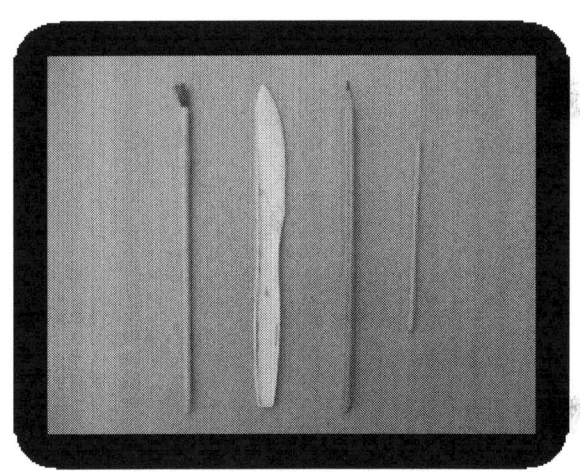

Plastic knives with the serrated edges trimmed using scissors and sharpened on sand paper are a cheap alternative to a potter's fettling knife and more suitable for use by young children. They are used primarily for cutting lengths of clay but can be used as a spatula to smooth joints between pieces of clay.

For these knives choose a style which is flexible, that is one which will not splinter if bent too far, children seem to have the knack of finding any weakness in the equipment.

Pencils or pointed sticks, shown in the picture, are used for adding details such as eyes or hair to models or drawing patterns and designs on pots of all descriptions. The pointed stick shown was made from 3mm thick skewers used in cooking Kebabs. Cut the skewer to the length you need, I got three from one skewer, sharpen one end and round off the other end using sand paper. Note in the interests of safety that the point should be blunted if the modelling sticks or pencils are being used by young children.

Work Surfaces.

The work surfaces shown in this section are available from craft suppliers or wood suppliers.

The dimensions for larger models are 30 cm x 20 cm made from 3 ply for the personal work surface, or for simple figure modelling 20cm by 15cm is sufficient.

I have recently found that the plywood can be replaced by thin MDF which has the added advantage of not splintering when it is sawn and remains flat if kept reasonably dry when not in use.

Work surfaces need to be absorbent to allow release of sticky clay, you will find that it is difficult to remove wet clay from shiny plastic surfaces. The work surfaces should be used for clay modelling only, if they are covered in oils or paints they will lose the absorbency needed for clay work.

Section 1. Why it didn't work.

What goes wrong.

Incorrect bonding techniques.

Consider the drying environment.

Keep to a uniform thickness.

Don't make it too thin.

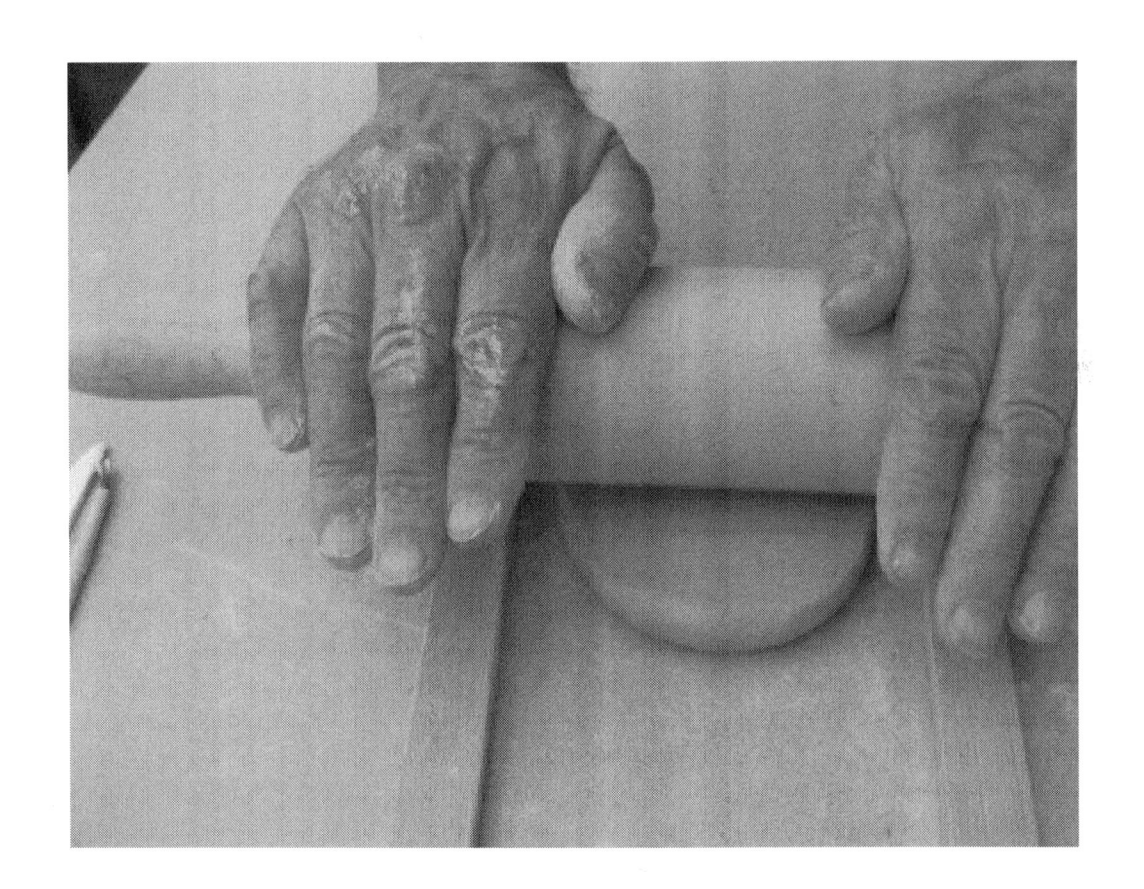

Why it didn't work.

Most teachers have either made clay models when they were at school or in class with their own pupils, models which invariably fell apart. The same applies to present day school children, they make models, stick the models together and when the models dry they fall apart at the slightest touch.

What goes wrong?

As models are being assembled the clay is soft and wet and by its very nature wet clay will stick to wet clay and students are misled in thinking that by just pushing the pieces together they make a successful bond.

However the problems appear when the clay is dry or drying, unless the correct 'bonding techniques' are used the drying joints will fall apart.

Incorrect bonding techniques.

Problems occur because the separate parts of the models to be bonded together are generally of varying sizes and thicknesses and so have varying drying times. In the process of drying the clay shrinks by 8% to 10% and as the pieces dry at different rates tensions are set up in the joints. The worst case scenario is to try to attach a wet piece of clay to a dry piece of clay, **it doesn't work** because the wet piece dries and shrinks while the dry piece has already shrunk, the joint will not stand the stresses.

With use of the correct bonding techniques the joints are able to stand the tensions and the model will remain as one assembly.

Consider the drying environment.

These problems are made worse if the drying environment isn't considered.

Models are placed in direct sunlight, or in draughts so one area of the model dries more quickly than the others.

Models are placed in direct contact with porous work surfaces which sucks the moisture out of the parts in contact while the other surfaces dry naturally but more slowly, all of which contributes to uneven drying times.

In each of these three situations one part of the model is encouraged to dry more quickly than the rest causing stresses and tensions in the model.

Keep to a uniform thickness.

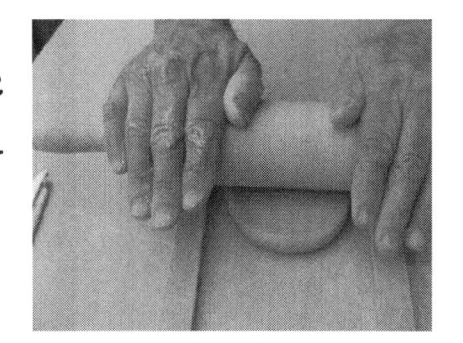

For this reason when building box-like structures we have adopted the technique of rolling out clay slabs to a uniform thickness by the simple use of identical slats of wood on each side of the slab which makes the rolled-out clay the same thickness as the slats. As the pieces are of a uniform thickness, and are being made at the same time from the same block of clay the shrinkage of the pieces is similar throughout the structure and with the correct bonding techniques the joints will be firm and strong.

Don't make it too thin.

The reason for this comment is to explain the major pitfall of thin clay. When thin clay is still moist it is safe to handle however when it is dry it is extremely brittle and breaks with the least provocation.

This also explains why I have included a section called '**make it chunky**'.

Section 2. How to make it work.

Correct techniques.

Slip, three methods to produce it.

Water containers.

Brushes.

Crosshatching.

Pressure and twist.

Slip.

Slip is a mixture of clay and water and there are several methods of creating it in various amounts. The production of slip is explained and discussed in 'Thirty Steps to Clay Modelling.

Slip is used in conjunction with crosshatching and pressure to help join two pieces of clay together, it can be likened to our glue or cement and is essential in bonding clay.

The creation of **slip** is an important part of joining together two pieces of clay

It is important to remember that the slip that you use must be produced with the clay that you are using to make the model, because when the models are fired the slip will fire to the same colour as the clay, slips produced from other clay will invariably fire a different colour and will show as a seam against the base clay.

Produce slip, method one.

I have found that the way to produce slip in volume is to first dry chunks of clay, of any size and when the clay has dried place it in a container and cover the pieces with water. After a few minutes you will see the clay starting to dissolve as the result of rehydration of the dry clay with the water which is breaking down the crystal lattice of the dry clay. As you can see from the picture in this section the edges of the clay are crumbling and making the water cloudy, this 'slaking down' of the clay will continue until the clay has completely dissolved.

The slip can now be produced by stirring the clay and water into a paste, the consistency depending on what you want to make. For joining pieces of clay together a thick, custard like consistency is practical. Remember you can always stir in a little water to adjust the mixture.

Produce slip, method two.

Most projects demand slip and a simple way to create it is to add water to a container of wet clay pieces and use a stiff brush or strong table fork to break down the clay and with sufficient energy slip will be produced.

Squashing the clay with the fork and rubbing the stiff bristles, laden with water, across the clay breaks down the clay and makes the slip.

Continue rubbing and adding water until the desired consistency is achieved.

Produce slip, method three.

The simplest way to produce slip, which is generally only used on small projects is to use a rough brush to apply water to the parts to be joined together. Both surfaces must be rubbed vigorously with the brush and water until sufficient slip is created on each surface.

This technique is usually adopted in modelling making the slip 'in situ' that is only on the surfaces to be bonded.

Clay surfaces at these points turn into slip, adding more water to make extra slip. Don't be afraid to make too much slip, it squeezes out of the joints as you apply pressure and the any excess can be wiped away with finger pressure around the joint, which also tends to strengthen the joint.

If clay modelling is a regular activity containers of pre-prepared slip can be kept available as a school resource. Containers can be simple recycled plastic tubs, each one needs a secure air tight lid to keep the slip moist when it is not being used.

In this case the stiff brush is used to apply the slip to the joints, roughing up the joints at the same time.

You may have noticed that I always refer to joints in the plural as you always apply slip to each surface to be joined.

Water containers.

I have always preferred plastic containers for use in clay modelling, they are light, easily cleaned and can be stacked together for easy storage. For years I have used recycled butter/margarine tubs.

Plastic containers also have the advantage of not smashing when dropped as would happen with a glass or ceramic container, a plus for reasons of health and safety.

One trick learned in the allocation of water containers is to add a small amount to each container, there is less to spill and less to mop up. Extra water can be always added as required.

Once again a collection of suitable plastic containers can become a school resource.

Brushes.

Brushes used in the preparation or application of slip needn't be expensive, in fact the cheaper brushes with stiff plastic bristles are ideal for clay work. Rubbing the clay surface with stiff bristles helps to break up the surface effectively making a larger surface area to be bonded together.

This type of brush for use with clay is virtually indestructible, they don't lose bristles and generally improve with age

Stiff brushes give an extra advantage of roughing up the surfaces as well as creating the slip helping the surfaces bond together. If the brush is really rough it could obviate the need to crosshatch all together.

However take care not to rub away too much clay making it too thin or causing, one piece to sink into the joint of the mating piece of clay.

Crosshatching.

What and why do we crosshatch?

Crosshatching or scoring is a technique used by potters and clay modellers to facilitate, in conjunction with slip and pressure, the successful bonding of two pieces of clay. Both surfaces to be joined must be cross hatched.

The effect of crosshatching is to break up the clay surfaces to be bonded allowing the water or slip to penetrate deeper into the clay.

This creates a larger and

14

deeper area of slip and larger malleable areas of clay which, when pressed together, will bond and recombine into one piece of clay at the boundary of the joints.

The analogy of this process is '**welding**' when two pieces of metal are fused together recreating one piece of metal in the jointed areas.

How do we crosshatch?

Crosshatching or scoring is generally carried out using the point of a plastic or metal knife as you reach the stage of bonding two pieces together.

Crosshatching patterns can be simple '**#**' signs for joining small areas, to larger areas of crisscrossed scoring covering the whole of the surfaces to be joined.

Alternative methods include a metal kidney with serrated edges, toothed plastic strip from a cling film dispenser and even a domestic fork. The tools suggested are used to break the clay surface to allow deeper penetration of slip.

These three alternatives would generally be used on larger areas of crosshatching while the knife points are used in more controlled situations.

Knives are held as though you were using a pencil, drawing the pointed edge of the blade through the surface of the clay in a regular pattern of lines, crosses or diamond shapes covering the areas to be joined together.

In order to quickly cover larger areas the multi toothed devices are held between your thumb and two or three fingers placing as much of the toothed device in contact with the clay surface as possible. Draw the tool across the surface in two or three directions to create as much scored surface as possible, take care not to weaken the overall structure of the model by making the clay too thin.

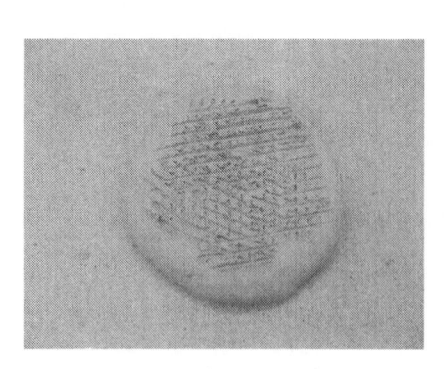

In the case of larger surfaces care must be taken to eliminate air bubbles between the surfaces when pressing them together which could cause a catastrophic release of pressure as the bubbles expand in the firing process.

When do we crosshatch?

Another common situation of crosshatching occurs in the building of box like models, house shapes or pencil pots as in the still photo shown, when the cross hatching is a series of crosses cut into the surface and edge to be joined.

Crosshatching should be carried out as soon as the pieces to be joined have been made so that the clay doesn't have time to start drying out, that is when the clay is still wet and malleable.

Ideally pieces of clay to be jointed should be made from the same block of clay at the same time and in the same stage of drying. If this is not possible the pieces should be wrapped in plastic or placed in plastic bags, made airtight and stored in a cool moist atmosphere until they are needed.

Pressure and twist.

Of the skills applied in bonding together two pieces of clay applying pressure to the joint is the most important.

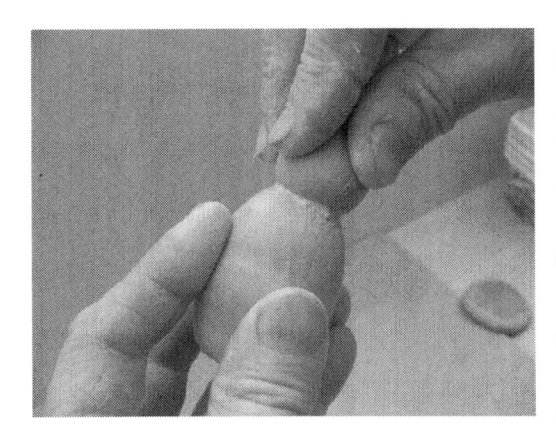

Using slip and crosshatching will help to stick the parts together but without pressure the joint will not bond together firmly and is less likely to survive the stresses of the drying process.

I have combined the action of applying pressure with the twisting action. Applying twist at the same time as applying pressure helps to recombine the malleable clay at the joints into **one bonded piece.**

Twisting entails a slight left to right rotation of round objects such as head to body.

When applied to a long thin joint one piece is slid or rocked backwards and forwards a few mms along the line of the joint – in all cases combined with pressure through one piece into the next piece.

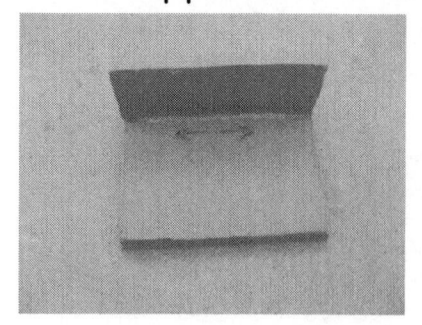

Finally, finishing a model, finger pressure around or along joints completes the process of reforming the clay back into one mass at the joints. In the picture of a frog shown, blending the underside of the foot back into the body makes a much more secure joint. This is just as important in sealing slab pot joints along the whole length to strengthen the structure.

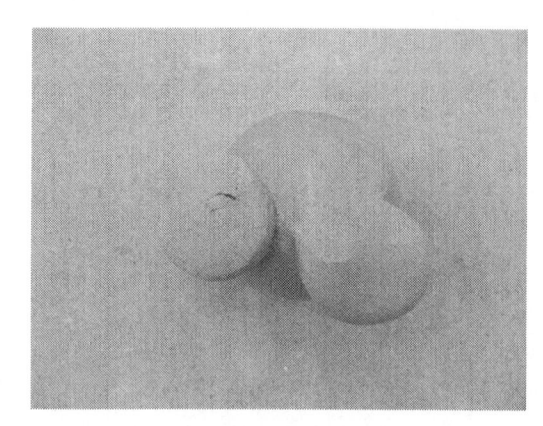

Section 3. Good practice techniques.

Make it chunky.

Add a base.

Add a support.

Why should we weigh clay.

Recommended storage techniques.

Assemble the largest pieces first.

Make it chunky.

When I say 'make it chunky' I am pointing out that the joining together of robust figures gives you a much better chance of making successful joints than jointing skinny pieces. As I pointed out in the first section handling thin pieces of clay, especially dry clay, is fraught with problems as thin dry clay is very brittle.

Figures with more substantial limbs and bodies are more likely to stay bonded together than their thinner counterparts which demand different techniques which we will cover later in this section.

Chunky figures give you larger surface areas to bond together.

Keep away from point contacts, if a limb or a branch needs to stick out then the contact area of the joints must be strong enough to support the clay extending from the main body of the model.

As a general rule in modelling there must be sufficient clay at each point to support the weight of clay above that point. For example when attaching a neck and head to a body the neck must be strong enough to support the head. Mushrooms need a sturdy stem and trees need a strong trunk.

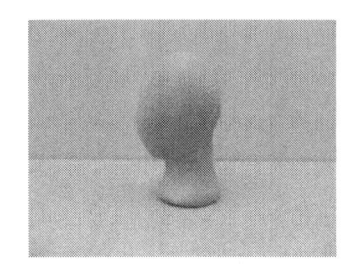

We have adopted techniques in clay modelling which help to overcome some of the problems mentioned.

An arm attaches to a person at the shoulder which is effectively a weak spot in a clay figure, to make it stronger attach the full length, or a portion of the arm to the body as demonstrated in the picture.

Add a base.

Models of animals and figures, especially ones with spindly legs, can be made more robust by the simple expedient of adding a base. The picture of the pig demonstrates this technique- the tail is pressed onto the body with slip and the four legs are attached to the base making the overall structure stronger and more stable.

Most model animals would benefit from fitting a base, the alternative is to make the animal seated or lying down and attaching the folded legs along the body.

Another variant on fitting a base is the Meerkat model. Without the base the back legs and the tail would be vulnerable however the addition of a simple base added by pressing the crosshatched underside of the body and the base together with slip on both makes for a more cohesive model.

Add a Support.

Spindly legged figures - even match stalk men - can be accommodated in clay modelling by incorporating them into a scene on a slab of clay in the form of a tile or a plaque.

The picture of a goalkeeper combined with impressed patterns is a simple example of this method of creating scenes. As a stand-alone clay figure the goalkeeper is a no-hoper, with a background the world is his oyster. He can be made to do anything, sports, dance and a

22

scene from a play are possible and as I mentioned match stalk men become viable.

Invertebrates and insects have spindly legs and thin wings which can be attached to a tile or if a 3D model is required the legs of a spider or octopus can be draped over a twig or a rock and with slip in the contact areas will be firm and safe from breaking from the model.

The alternative is to apply the body to a tile or to a rock as a base and draw the legs from the body into the tile. The picture of the ladybird is an example of this method.

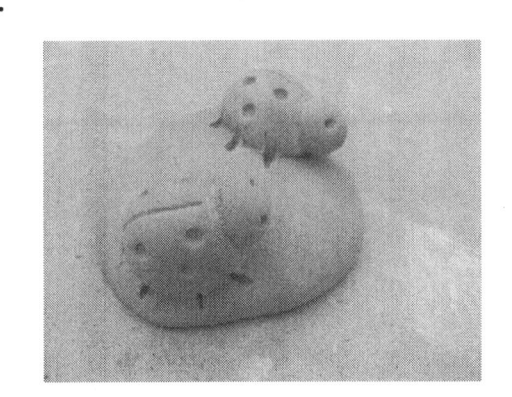

Finally a combination of base plus support can be developed where 3D models of say mushrooms may be attached to a base and connected to each other to form a stable group. This of course could be extended to dancers and groups of figures and animals, as long as they support each other. With such groups fixed together with a base then endless combinations are practicable and possible.

Why should we weigh clay?

There are several reasons for a potter to weigh clay the main one being repeatability.

By this I mean that if you want to produce models all the same size and dimensions the simplest way is to start with the pieces the same weight.

Over the years I have found that this strategy backed by templates produces models of uniform size.

I developed the strategy soon after we began teaching in schools. As I designed a particular model, for example a Roman Soldier, I assembled the model loosely, that is without slip, and when I was satisfied with the proportions I stripped him down to his component parts and weighed and measured each one.

To simplify the weighing process and to limit the number of pieces we needed to weigh if there were two or more on the model, for example arms, I noted double the weight of one and made two from the extended template. This also adds an element of judgement and measuring skills into the exercise for the students.

This is demonstrated in the practical exercise included in this tutorial which involves making four legs for the pig from one piece of clay.

If you wish to make several identical **thumb pots** use the strategy of weighing the first one made, then create a suitable template from the model showing diameter and height, your thumb pot can be repeated as many times as you wish. This will also help when you are joining thumb pots together to make a hollow model, the two parts will be identical making it easier to mate the edges.

This also applies to **coil pots,** if you want a straight and even coil pot weigh each piece of clay and as you roll the coils measure them against the template or ruler to keep them identical, don't be tempted to cut bits off- the resultant coil will be thinner than intended. To adjust the length press the ends until you get the correct length.

Recommended storage techniques.

Keeping your clay moist.

Complementary to the weighing of clay is to keep clay in airtight plastic bags, this keeps your clay moist and soft.

Always keep bulk clay in a sealed bag, and in a dark cool storage area, and for longer term storage try to double-bag it, that is keep it in two airtight bags.

Sealed to keep it moist, cool to help with keeping it moist and if possible dark to limit the growth of fungus which is accelerated in direct sunlight.

Note, the clay could be stored in a black bag to achieve both the double bagging and the darkened storage criteria.

Short term storage is achieved by keeping clay to be used in modelling in a plastic bags with the neck twisted to exclude the air.

When working with groups the clay should be prepared prior to the session. In fact the weighing and preparation could be used to give students practice in counting and weighing.

Preparation consists of weighing out the pieces and sealing the clay, for a specific purpose, in a plastic bag to keep it moist.

Identify the contents of each plastic bag using an indelible marker pen to add words or initials describing the intended use of the clay pieces in the bag. For example "**h**" on the bag could denote that the pieces in that bag were meant to be used for making the head.

Assemble the largest pieces first.

When making a model we have found that the modelling is more successful when you work with the pieces of the model in descending order of size and thickness.

If you think about it this makes sense as the larger the piece the longer it will hold the moisture needed to keep it malleable, the smaller pieces drying more quickly and becoming too hard to mould and bend, and as I pointed out earlier it is difficult to make clay bond correctly if the pieces are at different stages in their drying process.

So we always start with the body, subsequently add the head, feet, arms ears and lastly the nose.

B & M Potterycrafts.

Important things to remember.

1. Brush stiff bristles rough up clay.

Acts like cross hatching and makes a better joint.

2. Water + Brush = Slip/Glue.

Don't paint water on, rub it to create more slip and two soft surfaces.

3. Always make slip on both surfaces.

Two softened surfaces blend together to make a strong bond.

4. Press/Slide sticky surfaces together.

Pressure reforms the clay into one piece.

5. Smooth joint with finger.

Again this rejoins the clay into one piece and strengthens the joint..

www.bmpotterycrafts.co.uk

Just use your imagination.

Enjoy your clay modelling while trying out these skills on the practice project which incorporates most of the techniques discussed.

B & M Potterycrafts

B & M Potterycrafts.
Modelling Figures in Clay.
Make A Round Pig.

B & M Potterycrafts.

Make a Round Pig.

Contents and sequence.

Roll a ball for the body.

Make and fit the snout.

Make eyes mouth and nose.

Make and fit the ears.

Make and fit the legs.

Make and fit the tail.

Make and fit the base.

Make a pig worksheet.

MAKE A ROUND PIG.

Roll a ball for the body.

Roll the clay between the palms of your hands, exerting sufficient force to remove any lumps or bumps. Don't be tempted to take the easy route to smooth the clay by rolling it on the wooden work surface as this removes moisture from the clay and could make it too hard for modelling. Any creases or cracks can be smoothed using the fingers.

Continue to roll the clay until the surface is smooth and the clay is the desired shape ie a ball shape.

Make and fit the snout.

Take the clay between the palms of your hand rolling the clay until you form a smooth ball. Flatten the ball slightly by squashing it on the palm of one hand with the thumb of the other hand.

Crosshatch a spot on the body and one side of the snout using the point of your knife to score the clay with a '**#**' mark to cover the area of the snout. Use the paint brush and water to create **slip** by rubbing the brush and water firmly into the crosshatch marks on both the snout and the body. Finally **press** the snout firmly onto the body.

*The creation of **slip** is an important part of joining together two pieces of clay. The water from the brush is rubbed firmly into the clay surface until it turns light grey this is the slip and act as our glue.*

Crosshatching is one of the keys to joining two pieces of clay. It consists of scoring the pieces in the areas to be joined. Use the point of the knife to score clay.

*The use of **pressure** is essential in successfully joining two pieces of clay when used in conjunction with crosshatching and slip.*

Make eyes, mouth and nose.

Use the pointed stick to make the pig's eyes and nostrils pressing the point into the clay to make clear holes. Next cut the mouth into the snout using the edge of the knife as shown in the picture.

Support the body in one hand whilst adding the details.

Make and fit the ears.

To make the ears first roll the clay into a short sausage, mark the middle and then cut it in half, roll the two pieces into two small balls and squash them in the palm of one hand with the thumb of the other hand.

Use the paint brush and water firmly rubbing the brush into the surface of the clay to make two patches of slip above the eyes where the ears are to fit. Also make slip on one side of each ear in the places where the ears will fix to the head.

Firmly press each ear into the patches of slip in the positions indicated in the picture. Note that the tops of the ears are level with the pig's back to make it easier for the pig to lie on his back while his legs are attached.

Make and fit the legs.

Take the clay in the palms of your hands and roll it onto a sausage shape, try to maintain a uniform thickness along the length of the sausage shape to give you legs of an even thickness. Check the length against the template and finally tidy up the ends by tapping the sausage shape on the work surface.

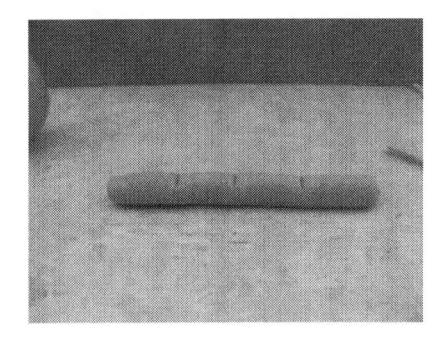

In order to make four legs of the same length first mark the sausage shape in the centre with your knife, when you are satisfied that the mark is in the centre cut the sausage shape cleanly in half. Repeat this process with the two pieces created, mark the centres, check the position of the marks and finally cut the pieces in half.

Reshape the legs into cylindrical forms before attaching them to the pig.

35

To fit the legs lay the pig on his back supported on his ears, make four patches of slip with the brush and water, one at each corner. Make slip on one end of each leg and press them firmly into place.

Stand the pig on his trotters, if necessary make adjustments to the lengths to make him stand correctly.

Make and fit the tail.

Roll the clay into a thin sausage shape to the length shown on the worksheet.

Use the brush and water to make a patch of slip at the back of the pig and make slip along the whole length of the tail to make it soft and pliable.

Press one end of the tail into the patch of slip leaving the tail standing erect then curl the tail with fingers and thumb and press the curly tail into the patch of slip.

Make and fit a base.

If you wish to make the model more stable and to add more skills to the modelling exercise the following paragraph will provide the information.

The first thing we have to do to make the base is to roll the clay into a smooth ball.

Take the ball in the palm of one hand and squash it flat with the other hand.

We need to make the base flat and large enough for the pig to stand on, not too big or the base will be too thin.

Having made the base to the correct size create four patches of slip with the brush and water on the base where the pig will stand. Make slip on the end of each leg, place the pig on the base with the ends of the legs in the patches of slip and fix it by pressing each leg firmly into place, don't press the pig as you will squash the legs.

B & M Potterycrafts.

Make a Pig Worksheet.

Clay.

Body.   80 grams.

Nose.   4 grams.

Ears.   4 grams.

Legs.   15 grams. | | | | | 7 cms.

Tail.   1 gram.

Base.   40 grams.

Printed in Great Britain
by Amazon